The Natural History Museum

Animal Close-Ups

Frogs and Snakes

Barbara Taylor

PETER BEDRICK BOOKS

McGraw-Hill
Children's Publishing

A Division of The **McGraw·Hill** Companies

Published in the United States in 2002 by
Peter Bedrick Books, an imprint of
McGraw-Hill Children's Publishing,
A Division of The McGraw-Hill Companies
8787 Orion Place
Columbus, OH 43240

www.MHkids.com

ISBN 1-57768-970-4

Library of Congress Cataloging-in-Publication Data is on file with the publisher.

Text copyright © Barbara Taylor 2002
Photographs copyright © The Natural History Museum, London 2002
Photographs by Frank Greenaway

The moral rights of the author have been asserted

Database right Oxford University Press (maker)

First published 2002 in arrangement with Oxford University Press.

1 3 5 7 9 10 8 6 4 2

Printed in Hong Kong

Contents

About this book

This book takes a close look at amphibians, which have smooth skin, such as frogs, and reptiles, with scaly skin, such as snakes. Reptiles usually live on land. Most amphibians go to the water to mate and lay their eggs.

I am a hopping frog.

I use my long, strong back legs to hop away from my enemies. I live on land and in the water. I breathe through my nose and my cold, wet skin.

I can jump more than six times my own length in one leap.

My toes are webbed, and that helps me to swim and move over boggy ground.

6

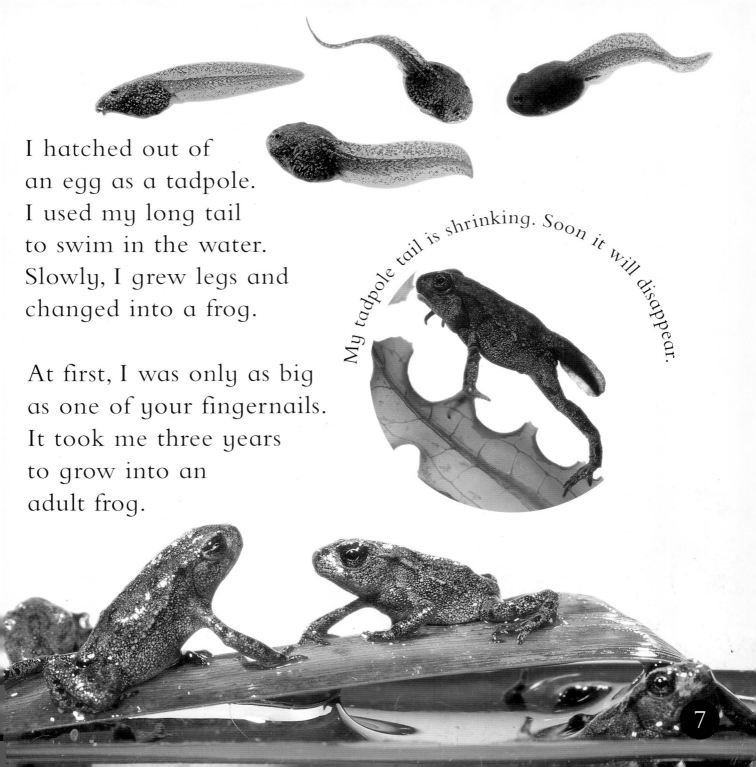

I hatched out of
an egg as a tadpole.
I used my long tail
to swim in the water.
Slowly, I grew legs and
changed into a frog.

At first, I was only as big
as one of your fingernails.
It took me three years
to grow into an
adult frog.

My tadpole tail is shrinking. Soon it will disappear.

7

I am a warty cane toad.

I live in damp, grassy places. I am bigger than an adult's hand. I can hear well, but I don't have ears like yours. My eardrum is a flat disc next to my eye.

I have lumpy glands full of poison behind my eyes.

I have a huge mouth, but no teeth. So I swallow my food whole. I gobble up insects, worms, frogs, and mice. I catch them with my sticky tongue.

My warty skin dries out easily, which is why I live in damp places. My legs are short. I cannot jump and swim as well as a frog.

My bulging eyes help me to keep a sharp look out for prey or danger.

9

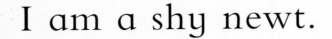

I am a shy newt.

I am called a palmate newt. I live on land some of the time but go back to the water to mate.

I have little specks of color on my skin.

My smooth skin is not waterproof. I have to live in damp places or I will dry out.

My back feet are webbed. They help me to swim.

I am about as long as an adult's finger.

In spring, I have a thread at the tip of my tail. I use my tail to attract female newts.

11

I am a deadly pit viper.

Beware of me! My venom is poisonous, and my bite can kill. I usually eat birds and bats. I hunt in the rain forest at night.

I hang by my tail from tree branches.

I have a bag of poison under the skin on each side of my head.

Every part of my body is covered by scales, even my eyes. The scales over my eyes are like see-through bubbles. They are called spectacles.

The holes under my eyes pick up the heat given off by the warm bodies of my prey.

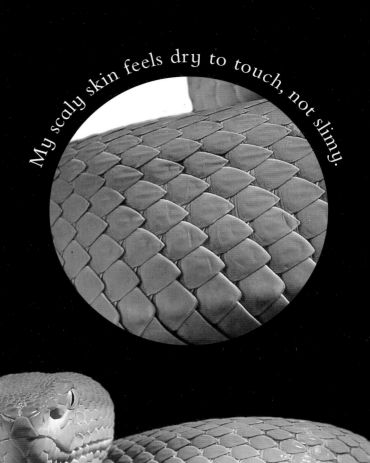

My scaly skin feels dry to touch, not slimy.

13

I am a spotted anaconda.

My spots help me
to hide as I wait in
the water to catch
a meal.

I squeeze my prey
to death in my
strong coils. Then I
swallow it whole.

The big scales on my belly help me to grip the ground.

14

I am a poisonous rattlesnake.

My forked tongue helps me taste and smell the air. I stare at you because I cannot blink or shut my eyes.

My rattle is made of old, hollow scales.

When I shake my rattle, it means, "Keep away, or I will bite you." My bite is poisonous.

15

I am a spiked iguana.

I am a type of lizard. I eat leaves, fruit, and flowers. I chop them up with my sharp teeth.

These thick scales help to protect me

I move my throat flap and my crest to display to other green iguanas. This is how I find a mate

My long toes and claws help me to climb trees.

I can use my long tail to strike my enemies. My green color helps me hide from them in the leaves.

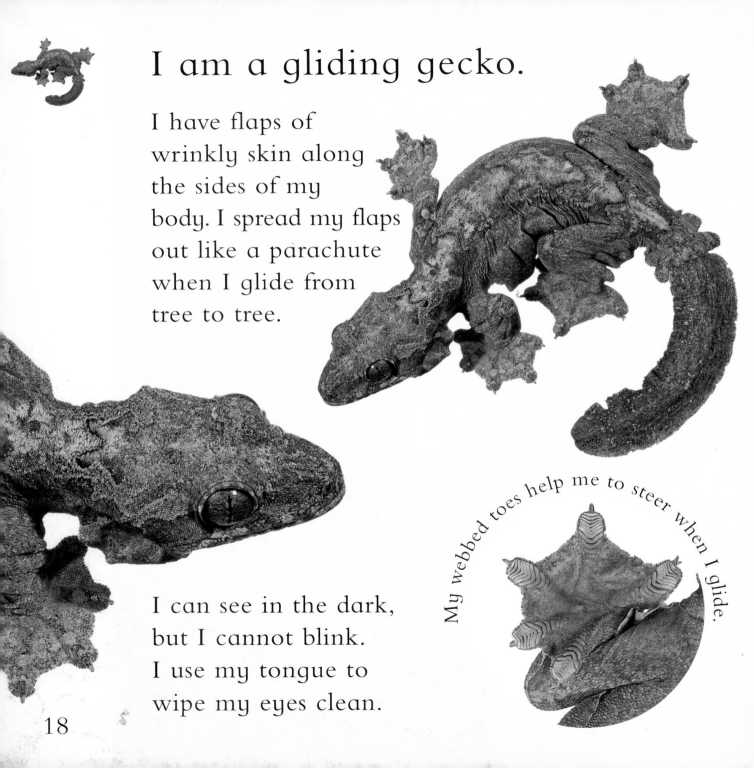

I am a gliding gecko.

I have flaps of
wrinkly skin along
the sides of my
body. I spread my flaps
out like a parachute
when I glide from
tree to tree.

I can see in the dark,
but I cannot blink.
I use my tongue to
wipe my eyes clean.

My webbed toes help me to steer when I glide.

18

I am a slow turtle.

My hard shell is like a
suit of armor. It protects
me from enemies. I live
in ponds and rice fields
in China.

My sharp claws help me to grip wet, slippery surfaces.

I have a top shell and a bottom shell.

I can pull my
head right
inside my shell.

I am a scaly caiman.

I am like an alligator,
but smaller. I live in rivers,
lakes, and swamps.

My beady eyes can even see in the dark.

I snap up fish with my strong jaws and spiked teeth.

When my old teeth fall out I grow new ones.

My back feet have webs of skin between the toes, like flippers. This helps me to swim.

Like a suit of armor, my bony scales protect me from attack.

Glossary

display Showing off parts of the body, to attract a mate.

lizard A reptile that usually has four legs, sharp claws, and a long tail.

mate One of a pair of animals that come together to produce young.

prey An animal that is killed or eaten by another animal.

scales Thin, hard, overlapping plates that protect the skin of fish and reptiles.

viper A very poisonous snake with a short thick body and a wide head.